THE BISON

BY
CARL R. GREEN
WILLIAM R. SANFORD

EDITED BY
DR. HOWARD SCHROEDER
Professor in Reading and Language Arts
Dept. of Elementary Education
Mankato State University

PRODUCED AND DESIGNED BY
BAKER STREET PRODUCTIONS
Mankato, MN

CRESTWOOD HOUSE
Mankato, Minnesota

LIBRARY OF CONGRESS CATALOGING IN PUBLICATION DATA
Green, Carl R.
    The bison.

    SUMMARY: Discusses the life style of the bison before it faced extinction, the period that almost killed it off, and the conservation efforts to restore the herds of North America's largest land animal.
    1. Bison, American--Juvenile literature. (1. Bison) I. Sanford, William R. (William Reynolds). II. Schroeder, Howard. III. Baker Street Productions. IV. Title.
QL737.U53G68   1985   599.73'58   85-6624
ISBN 0-89686-275-5 (lib. bdg.)

Interntional Standard Book Number:	Library of Congress Catalog Card Number:
Library Binding 0-89686-275-5	85-6624

ILLUSTRATION CREDITS:

Jeff Foott/Tom Stack & Assoc.: Cover
Lynn M. Stone: 4, 7, 18, 25, 26, 32, 35
Nadine Orabona: 8, 17
George Sanker/DRK Photo: 11
Library of Congress: 13
Bob Williams: 43, 45
Brian Parker/Tom Stack & Assoc.: 14, 22
Phil & Loretta Hermann: 21, 36, 38, 39
Jeff Foott/DRK Photo: 29
Tom Stack & Assoc.: 41

CRESTWOOD HOUSE
Hwy. 66 South, Box 3427
Mankato, MN 56002-3427

TABLE OF CONTENTS

A small herd of bison graze on a hillside in South Dakota.

Imagine a quiet morning in South Dakota. You're visiting Custer State Park. In the distance you see a cloud of reddish dust. What can it be? You move closer.

A large herd of dark brown animals stretches across the plain. Their hoofs seem to shake the ground. Soon you can see the animals more clearly. They have huge, shaggy heads and sharp horns. Large humps rise on their backs. "Bison!" you shout.

The bison are moving slowly, grazing on the tall grass. But wait. A running horse has spooked them. The herd breaks into a run in front of you. The 1,800-pound (818 kg) creatures crash through a grove of small trees. The nearby river doesn't stop them. They plunge in, bellowing wildly. The swimming bison don't notice the canoe that comes into their path. Sharp horns tip the canoe over. The people in the canoe have to swim for their lives.

A few minutes later, the last bison cross the river.

You've been watching one of the nation's last bison herds. But think of what you'd have seen a hundred years ago. The herds of those days would have taken several hours to cross the river.

How many bison were there? One pioneer wrote in 1869: "The herd was not less than twenty miles in width . . . and at least sixty miles in length, . . . two counties of buffalo! There might have been 100 thousand . . . or 100 million." Today, experts guess that at least fifty million bison once lived in North America.

Which is correct, bison or buffalo?

Most people look a little blank when you say, "bison." They blink, and then say, "Oh, you mean 'buffalo'!" Scientists, however, prefer the more accurate name of **American bison.** They point out that bison are not related to other animals called buffalos. Neither the African Cape buffalo nor the Asian water buffalo are anything like the bison.

It was early French explorers who caused the name problem. When they first saw the bison they called them **boeuf.** That was their word for "beef." Perhaps that made sense. Everyone on the plains hunted the bison for meat. In English, "boeuf" became "buffalo." For most of our history, people have used that name.

A bull, cow, and calf graze on an open prairie.

In this book, we'll use the scientific word, bison. If you want to think of these great animals as buffalo, that's okay. Their place in history is safe, no matter what you call them!

CHAPTER ONE:

The bison came from Asia

The American bison came to North America from Asia thousands of years ago. They crossed on a land bridge that existed between Siberia and Alaska during the ice ages. It is believed that the first Indians came to North America along the same route.

Plains bison at Wind Cave National Park in South Dakota.

Over the centuries, the bison developed into two types. One species is *Bison bison,* the plains bison. Most of the plains bison lived east of the Rocky Mountains and west of the Mississippi River. Smaller herds, however, ranged across many parts of the eastern United States.

The second species (a larger, shaggier animal) is called *Bison athabascae.* Also known as the mountain or wood bison, this type ranged through the mountains of western North America. Mountain bison lived as far north as central Alaska.

Bison hunting was the Indian's life

The western plains Indians in North America depended on the bison. Every part of the animal was useful. The hides were made into clothing and wigwams (tents). Indian children picked up dried bison droppings, called "buffalo chips." These made good fuel for campfires. Bison grease was used to protect the skin from the hot sun and the biting wind of the plains. Some bones were made into needles and tools. Rib bones were lashed together and covered with hide to make small, round boats. The hoofs provided glue, and bowstrings were made from the tendons.

Before the Spanish brought horses to the western plains in the late 1500's, the Indians hunted bison on foot. They would sneak up on a small part of the herd and kill the bison with spears and arrows. They wore bison hides to fool the bison. Later, when the Indians had horses, they could chase the running bison to make their kills. Sometimes they were able to drive a small herd of bison over a cliff. The tribes ate the meat fresh, or dried it to eat later as jerky.

The Indians killed only as many bison as they needed for food and hides. In the early 1800's, millions of bison were still roaming on the plains of North America.

The end of the big herds

It was the European settlers who brought the bison close to extinction. By the late 1800's, only 541 bison could be found in the United States. Eighty-five of these animals were living in the wild. A herd of two hundred lived in Yellowstone National Park. The other 256 were fenced in on private ranches.

This is a part of today's bison herd at Yellowstone National Park.

As long as the English and French settlers remained east of the Appalachians, the bison had been safe. Pioneer farmers who moved westward in the 1800's, however, saw the bison as a problem. The herds knocked down fences and ruined crops. In addition, they ate grass needed for cattle and horses. Killing the bison seemed a good way to solve the problem.

Greed also played a part in cutting down the number of bison. "Hide hunters" made good money by killing bison for their hides. The hides were made into "buffalo robes." These robes were prized by the Easterners for their warmth. Armed with rifles, the hide hunters could kill bison much faster than Indians armed with spears and arrows. The small herds east of the Mississippi were wiped out by the 1830's.

The large western herds were next. No bison were safe. Hide hunters along the Red River in the U.S. and Canada began collecting half a million robes a year. By 1850, nearly all the bison in the Dakotas, Minnesota, and nearby sections of Canada had been killed.

Railroads sped up the killing

The killing increased as the railroads moved west in the 1860's. The railroads and the new settlements that grew up along the tracks split the bison into Northern and Southern herds. The twenty million bison of the Southern herd were centered in Kansas. The larger Northern herd, with thirty million animals, roamed from Nebraska to Canada.

The U.S. government gave large pieces of prairie farmland to the companies that built the railroads. In turn, the railroads sold some of their land to new settlers. This was good business, because the farmers would later pay the railroads to carry their crops to market. But farmers and bison were natural enemies. The farmers fenced the prairie with barbed wire so their livestock would not wander away.

Because fences didn't stop bison, the farmers shot them on sight. They also shot bison for food and hides.

In the 1870's, the railroads found a new way to profit from the bison. Special trains took tourists out to the herds. The tourists shot the animals from the train windows. Usually, no one collected the meat or hides. Thousands of dead bison were left to rot. Other people, such as Buffalo Bill Cody, killed bison to feed the railroad workers.

Tourists used to shoot and kill bison from railroad cars.

Hides became big business

Technology also helped doom the bison. In the 1870's, a way to make bison hides into usable leather was found. The entire hide could be used. The best hides were made into coats. The poorest were used for belts to drive machines.

Millions of bison died to furnish hides for Eastern factories. The price of hides fell to $1.25 each. (Today that would be about $25.) Even so, by 1880, hide hunters had killed the last bison of the Southern herd.

The shaggy hair from bison hides was used to stuff mattresses.

Meanwhile, the hide hunters also attacked the Northern herd. A hide hunter who didn't bring in two thousand hides a year was a failure. Bones brought four cents a pound. Hoofs and horns were sold for six cents a pound. They were made into buttons, combs, and glue. Bison hair was worth more. At seventy-five cents a pound, it was used to stuff mattresses.

Prices fell as more bison were killed, but the hide hunters still made a good living. Most workers during that period earned very low wages. A railroad engineer, for example, earned twenty-five cents an hour. (By modern standards, prices were also low. Candy sold for only seven cents a pound.) Before long, the Northern herd was also wiped out.

Indian hopes died with the bison

The Indians knew they could not survive without the bison. As one Kiowa chief said, "Has the white man become a child that he should recklessly kill and and not eat? When the red men slay game, they do so that they may live and not starve." But white Americans refused to listen.

Angry Indians struck back. Warriors took to the

warpath and attacked white settlers. Much blood was shed. Nothing could slow down the killing of the bison, however. Some Indians joined in the killing, too. They saw a chance to trade bison robes for blankets, guns and whiskey.

Indian-haters praised the work of the hide hunters. General Phil Sheridan told Congress that "these men have done . . . more to settle the . . . Indian question than the entire regular army has done in the last thirty years." Sheridan was an old Indian fighter. He knew that the Indians could not live without the bison.

When the big herds disappeared, the Indians were forced to settle down on reservations. The days of the free-roaming Plains Indians ended with the death of the great bison herds.

The bison almost disappear

In the 1860's, naturalists had begun warning that the bison were close to extinction. Some western territories did try to stop the killing. Idaho outlawed bison hunting in 1864. Wyoming, Colorado, and Nebraska passed similar laws.

But most Americans weren't interested in saving wild animals. State laws that protected the bison seldom worked. If poachers (illegal hunters) were caught, they paid only a small fine. In 1894, poachers killed all but twenty bison in the Yellowstone Park herd. The U.S. Congress finally decided to protect the bison. A law was passed that put the bison under federal protection.

Conservation efforts pay off

Conservation is the belief that we must protect our natural resources. To some people, natural resources mean only rivers, minerals, and trees. Conservationists believe that the bison and other wild animals are also a valuable resource. The 1894 law was part of this new conservation movement.

The bison were not saved just by laws, however,

In Custer State Park, South Dakota, bison are provided a place of safety.

but by people. In 1901, "Buffalo" Jones was put in charge of the tiny Yellowstone herd. The herd soon grew in size. A writer named Ernest Baynes also stirred up interest. He wrote articles and letters about the killing of the bison. The American Bison Society was organized because of his efforts.

In 1907, fifteen bison rode a railroad car to Oklahoma. A crowd cheered as the bison were set free on a protected range. This was the Wichita Mountain Wildlife Refuge, set up by an act of Congress. The Bison Society bought land for another herd in Montana. In 1912, a range was set up in Nebraska. Two national parks were also opened in South Dakota. Slowly, the protected herds grew in size.

Some private citizens also did what they could to preserve the bison. Pete Dupree and James Philip raised bison in South Dakota. Their herd started with only five calves. Experts believe that most of today's bison are related to the Dupree-Philips herd.

Thanks to these conservation efforts, you can still see bison today. Now let's take a closer look at these interesting animals.

Thanks to "Buffalo" Jones, there is now a large herd of bison in Yellow Stone National Park.

CHAPTER TWO:

The largest North American animal

Here's a good trivia question. What's the largest North American land animal?

Some people will guess, "The grizzly bear." Others will say, "The moose." The correct answer: "The bison!"

How big is a bison? Male (bull) bison stand about six feet tall (1.8 meters) at the hump on their shoulders. The female (cow) averages five feet (1.5 meters) in height. Bulls are from nine to twelve feet in length (2.7 to 3.7 meters). Cows are two to four feet (.6 to 1.2 meters) shorter. The largest bulls tip the scales at three thousand pounds (1,360 kg). Most fully-grown bison weigh over a ton (907.2 kg).

Bison are herd animals

These large, powerful animals seem to enjoy company. Bison gather in herds. Only the very old bulls keep to themselves. Bison herds usually move peacefully across their grazing lands. But no one should count on the bison's good nature. Bison have been known to attack almost anything that moves, without warning or reason.

Horns, hump, and hair

People who see a bison for the first time are usually impressed by its horns, hump, and hair.

The smooth, sharp horns make good weapons. Bulls use their horns to defend the herd and to fight with each other. The horns also help the bison break through heavy brush. Running bison, in fact, can knock down trees up to six inches (15 cm) thick. This kind of hard use often chips and breaks the horns.

The horns grow from a large skull that is covered by almost two inches (5.1 cm) of heavy skin. The horns are hollow and curve out and up from the head. A typical bull's horns measure eighteen inches (45.7 cm) in length; a cow's horns are almost as long, but aren't as heavy. The world record horn can be seen at Yellowstone National Park — it's 23¼ inches (59.1 cm) long! At birth, a bison calf has stubby, one-inch (2.5 cm) horns. The horns are never shed, and grow in size each year.

A bison's horns are never shed.

Newborn bison look much like domestic cattle. Bison calves soon start growing a large hump, however. Formed of solid muscle, the hump rises above the spine. It begins near the rump, and reaches its high point above the front shoulders. Indians were fond of the tender meat from the hump.

Most of the year, a bison's coat of shaggy hair is dark brown. In late fall, the hair becomes thicker and fuller, to keep the bison warm in cold weather.

In late fall, the bison's shaggy hair gets thicker and lighter in color.

The hair also becomes lighter in color during the winter. In the spring, bison shed their heavy outer coats. This gives them a ragged, worn-out look. The bison scrape against rocks and trees to speed up the shedding.

A bison's coat is heaviest on the front part of the body. The hair on the head and hump may grow as long as twelve inches (30.5 cm). Farther back, the hair is often only two inches (5.1 cm) long. Bulls also grow a foot-long (30.5 cm) "beard" that hangs from their chins. Although most bison are dark brown, a few have been seen with white, gray, or cream-colored coats. Most calves are born with reddish-brown coats that darken as they grow.

Poor eyes, keen ears and nose

Like many grazing animals, bison see the world very dimly. They can spot movement, but not much else. Bison cannot focus on far-away objects. If you stand still, bison will likely not see you at all. The eyes are set in the sides of the head. Thus, bison can spot movement in all directions except to the rear.

Bison make up for poor eyesight with a good sense of smell. They use their big, wide noses to check the wind for danger. They can smell their enemies a mile (1.6 km) away. Bison can also pick up the faint scent of far-away water if the wind is right. They can even smell grass buried under a foot (30.5 cm) of snow.

Bison have equally good hearing. They pick up tiny noises, such as the crack of a twig under a person's foot. When that happens, they start running. Bison hear sounds long before a human would hear them. Knowing this, the Plains Indians would beat on drums when bison herds were nearby. The noise kept the bison at a safe distance from their camps.

Bison "talk" to each other

Bison use snorts, grunts and bellows to "talk" to each other. Calves, for example, make little "help me" grunts to call their mothers. Adults use a number of other sounds. Snorts and grunts warn others to stay away from calves, or to leave a bunch of grass alone. Different sounds serve as mating calls, or show a sense of fun during play. Loud bellows warn of anger and danger.

Bison also send signals with their tails. A tail moving back and forth, like a windshield wiper, means danger. When a bison is checking out something new and strange, it holds its tail straight up. The tail also makes a good flyswatter!

The bison in the background is using its tail as a flyswatter. The bison in front is dusting itself for more protection from insects.

A diet of grasses

Bison spend much of their time eating. Plains bison graze mostly on grasses. One of their favorite grasses has come to be known as "buffalo grass." Mountain bison also eat tender tree shoots, acorns, and berries. Like domestic cattle, bison have thirty-two teeth. The upper jaw has twelve molars (grinding teeth). The lower jaw has eight incisors (cutting teeth) and twelve molars. The mouth also contains a bluish-purple tongue. The tongue is long enough that the bison can clean its own nose.

Grass-eating animals, such as the bison, are known as ruminants. Like cattle, bison swallow their food before it is completely chewed. Later, they spit it up in small chunks called "cuds." Then they chew it a second time. The bison's stomach has four sec-

A bull lies down to chew its cud.

tions. This system enables them to digest the cellulose in the grass. Bison usually begin eating very early in the morning. Later, they lie down to chew their cuds. In the afternoon, they repeat the process.

Bison usually visit a waterhole sometime during the day. After drinking their fill, they may also seek out a salt lick. A salt lick is a place where an open vein of natural salt can be found on the earth's surface.

A good supply of these simple needs — grass, water, and salt — made much of North America a good habitat for the bison.

Bison once ranged across vast stretches of North America. Small herds were found in woodlands areas. But the biggest herds lived on the Great Plains. The plains provided the grasses, water, and space that large herds needed to survive. Most of today's herds are also found on the Plains.

Bison move in search of food

Long ago, the large bison herds moved great distances in search of fresh grasslands. This movement created a myth. Frontier settlers said that herds headed south in the winter, and returned north in the spring. Some people said that Canadian bison spent their winters in Texas! The map tells us that it's fourteen hundred miles (2,240 km) from Canada to Texas, however. Let's say the bison covered eight miles (12.8 km) a day, even though that would be fast for bison. It would have taken them five months of non-stop walking just to make the trip!

Modern research shows that bison actually move in any and all directions. They do not follow regular routes, as do migrating birds. They're just searching for fresh grasses to eat. Some herds do try to escape the fierce winter blizzards that sweep across the open plains. They move to wooded areas along the rivers. There they find shelter among the trees.

Speed and power

Bison herds usually travel at a slow walk. Herds walk along slowly, grazing as they move. They cover about two miles (3.2 km) a day. When alarmed, however, they shift into high gear. A running bison can reach a speed of over thirty miles (48 km) per hour. It can keep up this speed for thirty minutes or more. Bison are also sure-footed on their four hoofs. Despite their weight and size, they can climb steep river banks with ease.

Bison have four gaits — the walk, the trot, the gallop, and the bound. When they walk, the feet move in a regular pattern: right rear, right front, left rear, left front. To go faster, the bison breaks into a trot. During the trot, the feet move this way: right front and left rear together, then left front and right rear together.

When the bison wants to move faster, it goes into a gallop. The bison spreads its hind legs wide and springs forward. As it lunges ahead, the hind legs swing out ahead of the front hoofs. A galloping bison moves with great speed and power. The bound is a springy step seen most often when bison are playing. A bounding bison springs forward off all four feet at the same time, like a bounding deer.

Bison swim well enough to cross swift-flowing rivers. In deep water, only their humps, noses, and the top of their heads show above the surface. Even so, bison sometimes drown in icy rivers. If they run into ice on the opposite bank, they may not be able

Bison are good swimmers.

29

to pull themselves out. Their hoofs cannot grip the slippery ice.

Few natural enemies

The bison has few enemies other than humans. But a fast-moving prairie fire can sweep across the grasslands with blazing speed. Bison trapped by the flames will be killed. Others may be blinded by the smoke and heat. Blind bison can survive if they find a herd. Then they can follow the sighted bison to food and water.

Wolves were once a threat, but they are almost extinct today. Wolf packs used to chase down older bison who had strayed from the herd. After the bison could not run any more, the wolves moved in for the kill. For some reason, grazing bison often let a wolf creep in among the herd. The Indians knew this. They sometimes wore wolf skins so they could crawl among the herd and make their kills.

Only the grizzly bear and the cougar still hunt the bison, if they are in remote areas. Grizzlies are too slow to catch a running bison. They usually attack the sick or wounded in a herd. Cougars lie in wait, hoping to bring down a stray calf that might walk by.

Mites, lice, ticks, and other insects find homes in

the thick hair of the bison. These parasites do not seriously harm the bison, however. The "buffalo bird" (actually a cowbird) rides on the bison's back. Buffalo birds pay for their ride by pecking insects out of the bison's woolly hide.

Bison change a habitat

The large herds of long ago could change a habitat. They cut trails through woodlands from one grassy area to another. Along the rivers, the herds wore down the riverbanks. This provided natural crossing points called fords. Even, today, bison create new habitat by rolling and scratching in soft soil. This makes shallow holes about a foot deep called wallows. When the rains come, the wallows become small ponds.

Bison droppings are also important. The droppings fertilize the prairie grasses so important to the bison's life cycle.

Bison herds wear down the riverbanks, creating natural crossing points called fords.

CHAPTER THREE:

When left to themselves, bison live in harmony with their habitat. Their lives follow the cycle of the seasons. As with many animals, the bison's year begins in the spring.

Spring means new calves

The snow is melting as the spring sun warms the open plains. Winter has been hard. The bison moved

Bison calves are born in the spring. Each bison cow usually has a single calf.

from one snow-covered grazing area to another in order to find enough food. Now they snort with pleasure as they munch the spring's first tender grasses.

The year's first calves have already been born. Cows first give birth when they are three years old. A few cows have given birth to twins. This is unusual, as bison normally have single births. The cows carry their calves for nine months. The calves are born with their eyes open. They soon learn to stand on their unsteady legs. A little later, the hungry calves enjoy their first meal of rich bison milk. Within a few days, the calves and their mothers are ready to rejoin the herd. The young bison stay with their mothers until next spring.

The older bison look ragged. Their hair is coming off in patches as they shed their winter coats. The shedding makes their skin itch. They rub against rocks and roll in their wallows. A good layer of mud also helps protect them from insects.

The herd is usually a bit smaller in the spring than it was in the fall. Several old, weak bison died in a blizzard. Some others fell through the ice of a frozen river and drown.

Spring grasses grow taller as the days go by. Rich fields of buffalo grass will soon reach above the bison's heads. The good supply of grass helps the bison regain the weight they lost during the winter.

Summer brings fighting and mating

By late June, the calves stop nursing. They grow rapidly. Their new diet of grass agrees with them. The calves' reddish coats get darker and shaggier. Their knobby little horns are growing, and so are their humps.

The older bulls ignore the calves. They have started the mating season. Most breeding takes place in July and August. The bulls begin moving restlessly around the herd. They push each other, bellow, and roll in the mud and dirt more than usual. Tempers are short. The cows graze quietly, waiting to be chosen. Three-year-old bulls are ready to mate, but older males usually push them aside.

The strongest bulls try to keep ten or more cows to themselves. But these bulls must be ready to fight the younger males. A fight starts with two bulls trying to outstare each other. They paw the ground, then start to advance with heads down and tails up. Suddenly, they charge. They butt heads with a thud, trying to shove each other backwards.

Most fights are over quickly. The loser backs away. A few battles go on for hours, but bison are well padded. Serious injuries are rare. When the fighting is over, the winners return to their cows.

Two bulls battle on a frosty morning.

Mating takes place when the cows are ready.

Fighting and mating fill only a part of the bison's summer. On most days, the herd rises early. They like to graze while the grass is still wet with dew. When they've eaten their fill, they lie down. This is a time for chewing their cuds. Later, the herd may drink at a nearby waterhole. As the afternoon wears on, they return to their grazing.

Fall signals the end of lazy days

Fall means that winter's cold can't be far behind. The summer's grazing has added a layer of fat under the bison's skin. In addition, their hair is now longer and thicker. By October, the hides are at their best. That was the time when the Indians liked to take

Indians hunted bison in the fall, when the hides were at their best.

bison hides. The Indians also felt that bison meat tastes best in the fall. The tribes made large amounts of leather-tough jerky to use as food through the winter.

Many years ago, the herds often traveled hundreds of miles in search of food. Some wandered from place to place. Others made a large circle that took them back to where they began. The huge herds left a broad trail of grazed-over land behind them. Explorers who followed the trails found that they seldom went in a straight line. Bison trails, then and now, follow a logic known only to bison.

Today's smaller herds tend to stay within a limited range. The herd in Canada's huge Wood Buffalo Park, however, travels 150 miles (240 km) each spring in search of grasses — and then returns in the fall. Older males tend to travel on the outer edge of the herd. Perhaps the bulls are guarding the cows and calves.

When two herds meet, the bison stop some distance apart. Soon a bull steps forward from each herd. The two bulls paw the ground and butt heads. This battle almost always ends in a draw. When the fight is over, the two herds mix together peacefully.

Fall brings the danger of tornadoes and prairie fires. A "twister" will send the herd stampeding wildly. If the funnel cloud touches down near them, the winds will sweep many bison away to their death. Dried grasslands create another danger. Fires spread quickly. They are often set off by lightning strikes. Bison are fast, but they cannot outrun a prairie fire.

Winter tests the bison's toughness

Winter's shorter days change the bison's routine. The herds still move, but summer's lazy sunbathing

As winter gets closer, bison look for dried grasses in meadows.

is over. Food is harder to find, and the bison eat all through the short daylight hours. Each day, the herd seeks out meadows that still have dried grasses left from the summer.

Soon the first snows cover the ground. Domestic cattle will starve when grass is hidden beneath deep snow. But bison use their heads as snowplows. First they push their noses into the snow. Then they swing their heads back and forth. This clears a path to the grass beneath the snow. Over and over, the bison plow their way forward. In a few weeks, the snow and ice wear the hair away from the sides of their faces.

Bison seem to know when a storm is coming. They turn and face into the blizzard. Protected by their heavy coats, they can survive months of extreme cold that would kill domestic cattle. Canadian herds have survived cold of -60° F. (-50° C.). Heavy snowfalls add another danger. Bison trapped by large snowdrifts cannot move to new meadows. When the food supply runs out, the weaker animals will die. A warm spell can bring new problems for the herd. When snow melts and freezes again, a thick crust of ice forms on top. Bison who cannot break through this crust may die from lack of food.

Winter often kills the old, sick, and weak members of the herd. Only the strongest bison live to see the spring. This sounds cruel, but it is nature's way of making sure that only the fittest animals survive.

The bison "snow plows" with its head to reach grass under the snow.

CHAPTER FOUR:

A domestic animal

Some people still think the bison can become a domestic animal. Think of the heavy load a bison bull could pull! Bison refuse to be hitched to wagons, however. That idea was tried in the 1800's — and failed. No one has ever completely tamed a full-grown bison.

Most of the profits from raising bison today come from selling the meat. One ranch in Wyoming sells bison meat all over the United States. Many people who eat "buffalo burgers" say they have a "wild" taste. Bison meat is eaten mostly by people who are allergic to beef. These people don't mind the taste or the high price. They can enjoy a lean bison steak without getting sick.

Animal breeders have also used bison to create "cattalo." Cattalo are produced by breeding domestic cattle with bison. The breeders hope that these animals will inherit the bison's ability to live through cold winters. They've also found that cattalo fatten well on grass, unlike domestic beef cattle. At first, most of the cattalo bulls were sterile. Today, many of the bulls can produce their own cattalo calves.

More than a symbol

For most Americans, the "buffalo" is a symbol of the Old West. They've seen its picture on paper money, coins, and stamps. The bison appears on the

A "buffalo nickel."

state flags of Kansas and Wyoming. In Canada, the Royal Canadian Mounted Police seal has a bison on it. In addition, you'll find "buffalo" in the names of towns, rivers, and other places.

Thanks to conservation efforts, bison can still be seen in their natural habitat. Protected herds graze in parks and ranches in the United States and Canada. These animals breed well, and their numbers have been increasing. For the moment, bison are no longer in danger of extinction.

Today, almost twenty thousand bison live in the United States. Another fifteen thousand can be found in Canada. Many of these bison roam freely on open grasslands. Visitors can see them living much like the great herds did many years ago.

Perhaps you'll have a chance to see one of the herds. These big animals look rather tame at first. But don't try to get near them. The sharp-horned bison are still wild. An angry bull can pick up a horse and rider on its horns. Be especially careful if there are calves in the herd. The cows will charge at anything that gets too near their calves.

Luckily, you don't have to get close to enjoy the bison. The real thrill comes in seeing a herd roaming free. If you come early enough, you can watch the sunrise above hundreds of grazing bison.

Then try to imagine a herd that stretches all the way to the horizon. What a sight that must have been!

There used to be bison, "as far as the eye could see."

MAP:

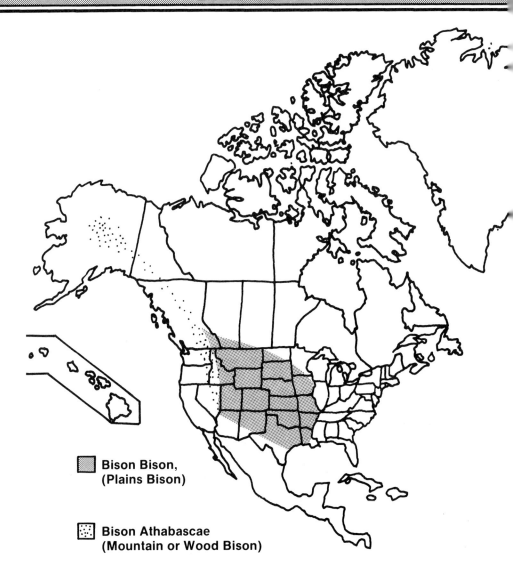

■ Bison Bison,
(Plains Bison)

▨ Bison Athabascae
(Mountain or Wood Bison)

INDEX/GLOSSARY:

WILDLIFE
HABITS & HABITAT

READ AND ENJOY THE SERIES:

If you would like to know more about all kinds of wildlife, you should take a look at the other books in this series.

You'll find books on bald eagles and other birds. Books on alligators and other reptiles. There are books about deer and other big-game animals. And there are books about sharks and other creatures that live in the ocean.

In all of the books you will learn that life in the wild is not easy. But you will also learn what people can do to help wildlife survive. So read on!